American Beauties

COLORING BOOK

Rendered by
CAROL SCHMIDT

Based on the artwork of
HARRISON FISHER

DOVER PUBLICATIONS, INC.
MINEOLA, NEW YORK

This truly unique coloring collection was inspired by the work of famed American illustrator Harrison Fisher (1877–1934). His work regularly appeared on the cover of *Cosmopolitan* magazine for nearly thirty years, and his "American Girl" drawings were considered the epitome of female beauty for nearly a quarter of a century. In this latest addition to Dover's *Creative Haven* series for the experienced colorist, artist Carol Schmidt has created 31 gorgeous portraits of late nineteenth- and early twentieth-century women, preserving the characteristics found in Fisher's "American Girl"—beauty, elegance, intelligence, and independence.

Copyright

Copyright © 2015 by Carol Schmidt
All rights reserved.

Bibliographical Note

American Beauties Coloring Book is a new work, first published by Dover Publications, Inc., in 2015.

International Standard Book Number

ISBN-13: 978-0-486-78203-4
ISBN-10: 0-486-78203-4

Manufactured in the United States by Courier Corporation
78203402   2015
www.doverpublications.com